There is NO *Hell*

The Book You Were Never Allowed to Think

Sherry Smith with Prestyn Smith

PRESTYN'S LIGHT

Published by:

Prestyn's Light Publishing
www.PrestynsLight.com
Email: hello@prestynslight.com

Edited by the Author

First Edition

ISBNs:

eBook: 978-1-967209-20-0
Paperback: 978-1-967209-21-7
Hardcover: 978-1-967209-22-4

Library of Congress Control Number:

For more information, visit: www.PrestynsLight.com

Dedication

For Prestyn.

The light that made thinking possible.

Epigraph

The Mind That Thinks Cannot Be Controlled

A Note on Spiritual Autonomy

*B*efore stepping into this message, I want to acknowledge something foundational. Every person has the right to believe what aligns with them. Spiritual autonomy is protected both by our Constitution and by the nature of the soul itself. Nothing in these pages seeks to impose belief or challenge another person's freedom. This is simply the truth as it has been revealed to me and the knowing that moves through my life.

Message from the Author

There are moments in life when truth does not arrive gently.
It arrives like a strike of clarity that rearranges everything you once believed.
This book was born in one of those moments.

I did not set out to challenge a doctrine.
I did not set out to confront a belief that shaped generations.
I simply allowed myself to think.
And once the mind begins to think, it becomes impossible to control.

What follows is not an argument.
It is not a debate.
It is not an attack on anyone's faith.
It is a clean examination of a claim that was never meant to be examined.

If this book finds you, it means you are ready for truth that does not rely on fear.
It means you are ready to think in a way you were not permitted to before.
And once you begin thinking for yourself, you cannot return to the world you were taught to accept.

This book is your permission slip.
Your mind will take care of the rest.

— Sherry Smith
with Prestyn Smith

Prologue: The Doctrine That Never Held

The idea of hell is one of the most powerful stories ever told.
It shaped cultures, controlled societies, guided behavior, and defined morality for centuries.
But a story becomes dangerous when it is accepted without thought.

Hell was never taught to be examined.
It was taught to be obeyed.
It survived because people were instructed to fear the question, not explore the answer.

Once you step outside the story, the entire structure collapses.
It cannot withstand logic.
It cannot withstand history.
It cannot withstand psychology.
It cannot withstand spiritual truth.
It cannot withstand the simple fact that the soul cannot be harmed.

This book does not fight the doctrine.
It simply reveals it.
And once something is seen clearly, it loses its power.

The doctrine of hell never stood on truth.
It stood on repetition.
And repetition is not evidence.

When the mind begins to think, the fear dissolves.
This is where the unraveling begins.

Table of Contents

Introduction

Most people never question what they were taught about hell.
Not because they agreed with it
and not because it ever made sense
but because they were trained to accept the fear
before they ever developed the ability to think.

This book exists for one reason.

To return your mind to you.

Not to give you a new belief
not to offer a new doctrine
not to replace one fear with another
but to give you the one thing you were never offered
when this idea first entered your life.

A chance to think.

When you remove fear
what remains is clarity.
When you remove repetition
what remains is awareness.
When you remove inherited belief
what remains is the truth your own mind can recognize.

This book does not ask for faith.
It does not require agreement.
It does not depend on doctrine.
It depends only on your ability to examine a claim
and follow the evidence
wherever it leads.

If you allow yourself to think
honestly
quietly
without fear
without pressure
without inherited assumptions
the doctrine of eternal punishment collapses
not through argument
but through understanding.

This is not a book about what to believe.
It is a book about what becomes clear
when you finally think for yourself.

That is all you need.

Now we begin.

The Moment the Truth Broke Through

I was washing the dishes when the thought arrived. No warning. No buildup. No sacred meditation or spiritual ritual. Just warm water, soap, a quiet mind, and a single truth waiting for the space to come through.

It came so clean and so direct that it stopped me.
Then I laughed.
I laughed the kind of laugh that breaks something open inside you.
Because the absurdity of it all landed with such clarity that my whole body responded.

The thought was simple.
Almost innocent.
Almost embarrassing to realize I had lived this many years without asking it.

If the soul has no body
what exactly is burning?

The moment that question formed, the entire story collapsed.
Not in pieces.
Not slowly.
Not after hours of contemplation.
It collapsed instantly.
Like a structure that only stood because no one ever touched it.

I laughed because it was so obvious.
I laughed because the spell finally broke.
I laughed because this fear that humanity carried for centuries could not survive one moment of actual thinking.

Not belief.
Not rebellion.
Not defiance.
Thinking.

Real thinking.
Honest thinking.
Unconditioned thinking.
Thinking without the weight of inherited fear sitting on top of it.

The entire doctrine of hell depends on one silent agreement.
That you do not think.
That you do not question.
That you do not look directly at the mechanics of the claim.

Because the moment you do
it falls apart.

A soul is not physical.
A soul has no skin.
A soul has no nerves.
A soul has no tissue to burn.
A soul has no lungs to inhale smoke.
A soul has no brain to register pain.

So what exactly is being burned
and how?

No one ever explained that part.
Because the doctrine was never designed to withstand examination.
It was designed to be absorbed without question.
It was meant to enter your mind before your thinking matured, before your awareness sharpened, before you had the capacity to stand back and say:
None of this makes sense.

That moment at the sink was the first moment I truly saw it.
I realized I had never been invited to think for myself about hell.

Not once.
Not in childhood.
Not in school.
Not in the culture around me.
The story was handed down as truth
but never presented as a claim that required thought.

The more I stood there with my hands in the water, the more ridiculous
the entire doctrine revealed itself to be.
Not because I wanted it to be false.
Not because I was rejecting something.
But because reality does not bend to fear stories and never has.

I saw clearly that the doctrine of hell is a structure built on human fear,
human control, and human storytelling
not on spiritual law.
Nothing about it matched the nature of consciousness.
Nothing about it aligned with the reality of the soul.
Nothing about it reflected the Source I am directly connected to.

And when something is not true
it cannot withstand a question.

This book is that question.
This book is for the person who has never been invited to think about hell
as a claim.
Not as a belief.
Not as a tradition.
As a claim.

A claim that demands:
What is the mechanism
What is the evidence
Who benefits
Who created it
Who enforces it
Why does it contradict every known spiritual law

Why does it collapse under the simplest inquiry
and why has no one asked these questions out loud.

You were taught a story.
You were never taught to examine it.

This book is the examination.
This book is the return of your own thought.
This book is the moment your mind remembers itself and steps out of captivity.

The spell breaks here.
And once it breaks
it never rebuilds.

Welcome.

The Mind Under Capture

What You Were Told Before You Could Think

*E*very belief that holds power over a person begins the same way.
It is given to them before they have the ability to question it.
Before critical thinking forms.
Before logic matures.
Before the mind knows how to evaluate claims.

This is how fear takes root.
Not through truth
but through timing.

Hell was not presented to you at a moment of intellectual maturity.
It was presented to you when your mind was still forming
when you trusted every adult voice
when you accepted every authority without examination
when you did not yet know how to think for yourself.

By the time your mind matured
the fear had already been installed.

This is not your fault.
It is by design.

The doctrine of hell depends on this early implantation.
If it were introduced to a fully developed, questioning mind
every part of it would be rejected for the same reason I laughed at the sink.
Because the moment you apply thought
the story collapses.

Beliefs handed to children do not need to make sense.
They only need to trigger fear
reward obedience
and create an emotional imprint deep enough to endure adulthood.

This is how the mind becomes captive without knowing it has been taken.

A captive mind is not chained by truth
it is chained by repetition.
It hears the same story so many times that it becomes familiar
and familiarity begins to masquerade as truth.

The tragedy is simple
you never stood a chance to evaluate hell.
You were introduced to it too young
too unprepared
too trusting
too open.

No one told you
You have a right to think
You have a right to question
You have a right to examine every claim placed in your mind
You have a right to reject fear
even if it was handed to you by people you loved.

Hell was not taught as a possibility.
It was taught as reality.
And because the mind of a child cannot distinguish fear-based fiction from
spiritual truth
the doctrine rooted itself where your thinking could not reach.

That is how the capture happened.

Not on the level of logic
but on the level of imprint.

A mind that was never invited to question will never know it is allowed to.

This chapter is the doorway to everything that follows.
Because before we dismantle hell
we must acknowledge the mechanism by which it entered your life.

Not through examination
but through implantation.

Not through truth
but through conditioning.

Not through spiritual understanding
but through fear.

This is where your liberation begins.

You were told a story before you could think.
Now you will think.
And the story will fall.

Fear Conditioning 101

*F*ear is the oldest method of control.
It does not require truth.
It does not require evidence.
It does not require logic.
It only requires repetition and authority.

Tell a child that fire burns
and they learn caution.
Tell a child that eternal fire burns the soul
and they learn obedience.

The difference is simple
one is reality
the other is fear conditioning.

Fear conditioning is a psychological process that bypasses thought
bypasses logic
bypasses evaluation
and goes straight into the emotional center of the mind.

Once fear is planted
the mind stops questioning.

Fear is the perfect tool for creating compliance
because fear promises something worse than disobedience ever could.
It tells you
If you do not follow
you will be harmed.
If you do not obey
you will suffer.

If you do not submit
you will pay.

This is not spirituality.
This is conditioning.

And hell is the most extreme form of fear conditioning ever invented.
It is fear stretched across eternity.
It is terror with no relief.
It is punishment with no pathway out.

It is designed to be so overwhelming that the mind never tries to examine it.

Fear can only survive where thinking ends.

This is why the doctrine of hell is introduced early
before the mind can question it
before the child can ask
Why would an infinite Source punish a soul eternally
What purpose would it serve
How would this produce growth
How does this align with love
What kind of law allows harm with no end
What kind of justice has no remedy
What kind of truth cannot be examined.

A thinking mind weakens fear.
A questioning mind destroys it.

So fear is delivered before thinking.
Before questioning.
Before the mind matures enough to recognize manipulation.

This is how the doctrine of hell is kept alive.
Not through truth
but through psychological force.

Fear conditions the mind to behave.
Fear conditions the mind to obey.

Fear conditions the mind to silence its own questions.

And fear conditions the mind to call the conditioning
faith.

When you confuse fear with faith
the prison becomes self-maintained.

You do not need chains
because the belief becomes the chain.

You do not need enforcers
because the fear enforces itself.

This is how an idea with no evidence
no logic
no spiritual foundation
and no coherence
has survived for centuries.

Not because it is true
but because it was planted before you knew how to think.

Once fear has shaped the foundation of a person's mind
they become loyal to the fear
not the truth.

This book will reverse that.

Fear will no longer be your authority.
Truth will.
Thinking will.
Awareness will.

Hell only survives where fear lives.
And fear only survives where thinking has been denied.

You are thinking now.
The conditioning ends here.

The Mind That Never Questioned

*T*here is a moment in every person's life when they realize something profound.
A realization so simple that it almost feels embarrassing.
A realization so obvious that it should have been seen long ago.

The realization is this
You never actually questioned the doctrine of hell.

Not once.
Not fully.
Not honestly.
Not outside of fear.

You may have doubted it.
You may have felt uncomfortable with it.
You may have wished it were not true.
You may have pushed it to the back of your mind.

But you did not question it.
Not in the way truth demands.
Not in the way reason requires.
Not in the way a free mind is capable of.

Why
Because the idea of hell was never presented to you as something to examine.
It was presented as something to accept.

And when a belief enters the mind as unquestionable
the mind learns to treat it as unthinkable.

Fear does not just silence the mouth
it silences the mind.
It teaches you that even forming the question is dangerous.
It convinces you that the doubt itself is a violation.
It warns you that thinking too deeply is risky.

The doctrine survives not because people believe it
but because they are trained not to think about it.

A belief that cannot survive a question
must survive by preventing questions.

This is why the moment you finally do think
the structure falls apart.

Because hell only exists in a mind that has been taught to avoid thought.

Once thought is allowed
the collapse becomes immediate.
The logic dissolves
the coherence disappears
the fear loses power
and the claim begins to reveal itself as nothing more than a story repeated
for so long that it masqueraded as truth.

Think about how strange it is
that you learned about eternal fire
eternal suffering
eternal punishment
eternal consciousness in pain
but were never encouraged to ask
How
Why
By what mechanism
Under what law
Based on what evidence

For what purpose
Maintained by what intelligence.

This omission is not incidental.
It is essential to the doctrine's survival.

If people were taught to think about hell
they would reject it in minutes.
If children were taught to question fear
fear would lose its power.
If adults revisited their own beliefs with the mind they have now
they would walk away from inherited illusions with ease.

The doctrine depends on your silence.
It depends on your obedience.
It depends on your lack of examination.

It depends on a mind that never questioned.

But the moment you do question
the moment thought returns
the moment awareness wakes up
the doctrine cannot stand.

This book is your permission to think.
Not with fear.
Not with guilt.
Not with inherited limitations.
With your full mind.
With your full awareness.
With the clarity that was always yours.

The moment you begin thinking
hell ends.

The Questions You Were Never Allowed to Ask

*E*very belief reveals its truth or its weakness through the questions it can survive.
Any claim that collapses under questioning was never truth.
It was conditioning.

Hell does not collapse because of disbelief.
Hell collapses because of questions.

Not complicated questions.
Simple ones.
Questions any child could ask
if they were allowed to.

But you were never allowed to.
Not directly
not out loud
not inwardly
not without the fear of punishment echoing behind the thought.

This is why the doctrine survived for centuries.
Not because it made sense
but because you were taught never to test it.

So the first step in liberating the mind is also the simplest.
Ask the questions you were never permitted to form.

Begin with the most basic.

If the soul has no body
what exactly is burning.

If the soul has no lungs
what exactly is inhaling smoke.

If the soul has no nerves
what exactly is registering pain.

If the soul has no tissue
what exactly is being damaged.

If the soul is not physical
why is the punishment described in physical terms.

If consciousness is nonphysical
how can it be tortured by physical fire.

If divine intelligence is infinite
why would it create a system dependent on fear.

If we are made by Source
why would Source destroy its own creation.

If growth is the purpose of incarnation
what growth is possible in eternal suffering.

If free will is sacred
how is an irreversible eternal punishment compatible with spiritual law.

If eternal punishment is real
why is there no evidence in any spiritual realm
any spiritual communication
any metaphysical observation.

These questions do not require rebellion.
They require honesty.
They require presence.
They require intellectual courage.

Every single one of these questions exposes a fracture in the doctrine of hell.
Not one of them has a coherent answer.

Not one of them survives examination.
Not one of them leads to truth.

And if a belief collapses under simple questions
it is not a belief you were meant to carry.

The most revealing question of all is this
Why were you never encouraged to ask any of these questions.

The answer is simple.
Because the doctrine cannot withstand them.

Truth invites questions.
Truth welcomes examination.
Truth grows clearer the more you think about it.

Fear does the opposite.
Fear warns you not to ask.
Fear threatens you for thinking.
Fear convinces you that silence is safety.

This chapter is your return to thought.
Your return to permission.
Your return to the questions that should have been asked long ago.

A claim that cannot survive questions
cannot be truth.

Ask the questions
and the illusion ends.

The Moment Thinking Begins the Story Ends

*T*here is a moment, subtle at first, when a belief that once felt enormous suddenly becomes small.
A moment when something that once felt powerful begins to lose its weight. A moment when the mind finally lifts its head and sees the story for what it has always been.

Not truth.
Not spiritual law.
Not divine instruction.
A story handed down before you could think.
A story maintained through fear.
A story protected by silence.
A story inherited, not examined.

This moment is the beginning of your freedom.

Because once thinking begins
the spell ends.

Hell is not dismantled by force
it is dismantled by thought.
By presence.
By clarity.
By a mind that finally recognizes its own power.

The truth is simple
hell only exists in a mind that has never examined the claim.
The moment examination begins
the doctrine has no ground left to stand on.

It cannot explain its mechanics.
It cannot explain its purpose.
It cannot explain its origin.
It cannot explain its logic.
It cannot explain its contradictions.
It cannot explain its absence from spiritual law.
It cannot explain why the soul would be punished for eternity when eternity serves no evolution.

It cannot explain anything.

The doctrine depends on your silence.
Not your belief.
Your silence.

Belief without thought is obedience.
Belief with thought is clarity.

And clarity has no use for fear stories.

The truth is that hell collapses under the simplest act
the act you are performing now
the act the doctrine hoped you would never perform
thinking.

Not emotional thinking
not rebellious thinking
not angry thinking
clear thinking.

Pure, grounded, direct thought.

When thinking begins
questions form.
When questions form
the structure weakens.
When the structure weakens
truth comes in.

When truth comes in
fear cannot survive.

This is why the doctrine tried to reach you before your mind matured.
Because a mature mind does not accept the impossible.
A mature mind does not surrender itself to fear.
A mature mind does not confuse punishment with divinity.

A mature mind sees.

And once you see
the story is no longer convincing.

This chapter closes Part I because you are no longer the person who received
the doctrine.
You are the person who is now evaluating it.
You are the person who sees the psychological design.
You are the person who understands the timing.
You are the person who recognizes the conditioning.

Hell does not end when you stop believing in it.
Hell ends the moment you start thinking about it.

That moment is here.

The Claim

Defining the Claim

$\mathcal{B}$efore you evaluate anything
you must define it.
Every attorney knows this.
Every investigator knows this.
Every thinker knows this.

If you cannot define a claim
you cannot test it.
And if you cannot test it
you cannot trust it.

So let us state the claim exactly as it has been taught for centuries
stripped of poetry
stripped of emotion
stripped of inherited imagery.

The doctrine of hell asserts that

A nonphysical soul
enters a nonphysical realm
where a nonphysical intelligence
inflicts eternal physical torture
through physical fire
on an essence that has no physical form.

This is the claim.

Not the softened version.
Not the symbolic reinterpretation.

Not the metaphorical explanation that modern thinkers try to use to escape the absurdity.

This is the literal doctrine as taught to billions.

And the moment it is presented clearly
it collapses.

Because nothing about this claim aligns with anything we know about the soul
consciousness
energy
spiritual law
or even basic logic.

A soul is not physical.
Fire is physical.
Pain is registered through physical nerves.
Tissue burns because tissue exists.
Smoke suffocates lungs because lungs exist.
Heat damages matter because matter exists.

How does physical fire act upon a nonphysical entity.
How does a soul that cannot decay burn.
How does a consciousness with no nervous system feel pain.
How does an eternal essence undergo physical torture in a realm with no physics.

The claim is incoherent.
Not metaphorically incoherent
literally incoherent.

A spiritual punishment that relies entirely on physical mechanisms
while being applied to a nonphysical being
is a contradiction so complete that the doctrine fails before the argument even begins.

This is why the doctrine is never defined clearly.
Clarity exposes falsehood.

Precision exposes impossibility.
Definition exposes deception.

Once you define the claim
its impossibility reveals itself.

This chapter is simple
because truth is simple.
If you cannot define a claim coherently
you cannot defend it.
If you cannot defend it
you cannot believe it.
If you cannot believe it
the fear attached to it loses power.

Hell depends on vagueness
on imagery
on fear
on repetition
on emotional imprinting.

It does not depend on clarity
because clarity destroys it.

This is the moment the reader begins to understand
the doctrine was never meant to be defined
it was meant to be believed.

And a belief that cannot be defined
cannot be real.

The Impossibility of a Physical Punishment for a Nonphysical Being

*N*ow that the claim has been defined
we examine its mechanics.

If someone makes a claim
they must be able to explain how the claim works.
Every legal argument
every scientific theory
every spiritual truth
must answer one simple requirement
mechanism.

If a claim depends on a mechanism that cannot exist
the claim cannot be true.

So let us return to the doctrine.

It asserts that a nonphysical soul
is subjected to physical torture
by physical fire
in a physical way
for eternity.

Immediately one question rises
How.

This is the one question the doctrine cannot answer.
Not with logic
not with theology
not with metaphysics
not with any spiritual law.

A nonphysical essence cannot burn
because burning is a physical process.
Burning requires matter.
Burning requires tissue.
Burning requires oxygen.
Burning requires a nervous system to register pain.
Burning requires a body that can decay under extreme heat.

The soul has none of these.

So what exactly is burning
and by what mechanism.

The doctrine never answers this
because it cannot.

A soul has no skin
yet the story insists it blisters.
A soul has no lungs
yet the story insists it suffocates.
A soul has no nerves
yet the story insists it feels pain.
A soul has no brain
yet the story insists it processes endless suffering.

None of this is coherent.
None of this is possible.
None of this aligns with anything known about consciousness.

The doctrine only survives when the mind refuses to ask
How.

The moment you ask
the story collapses.

This is not interpretation.
This is not metaphor.

This is not poetic symbolism.
This is pure contradiction.

Fire interacts with matter.
A soul is not matter.
Therefore fire cannot interact with a soul.

The doctrine does not work.
Not spiritually.
Not logically.
Not metaphysically.
Not intellectually.

And this single truth dismantles the entire claim.

If the mechanism is impossible
the punishment is impossible.
If the punishment is impossible
the doctrine is impossible.
If the doctrine is impossible
the fear is unnecessary.

The moment you understand this
you step into a new reality.

A reality where you are no longer controlled by a threat
that never had the ability to exist.

The Evidence

Zero Evidence, Zero Foundation

A claim that shapes the destiny of billions demands evidence.
Clear evidence.
Consistent evidence.
Spiritual evidence.
Historical evidence.
Logical evidence.

Yet the doctrine of eternal torture has none.

Not a trace.
Not a record.
Not a demonstration.
Not a single verifiable source outside of the texts that introduced the claim.

Every true spiritual reality leaves patterns.
Every universal law leaves signs.
Every realm of consciousness produces consistent testimony across time and culture.

Eternal torture leaves nothing.

No spiritual record.
No metaphysical imprint.
No cross cultural consistency.
No universal agreement.
No recurring evidence across serious inquiry.
No documentation across the thousands of years of human spiritual exploration.

Nothing.

What exists instead is the repetition of a story
and the fear attached to it.

Fear is not evidence.
Repetition is not evidence.
Tradition is not evidence.
Authority is not evidence.
Emotion is not evidence.
Threat is not evidence.

The absence of evidence becomes even more powerful when you consider
what should exist if eternal torture were real.

If billions of souls were suffering without end
there would be metaphysical signs.
There would be spiritual communication.
There would be warnings from every corner of the world.
There would be cross cultural accounts.
There would be consistency across independent human experience.

Instead
there is silence where eternal torture should be.
A silence deep enough to expose the truth on its own.

across every continent
across every culture
across decades of scientific study
no verified report describes eternal punishment.

Not one tradition describes endless suffering with no possibility of transition.

If eternal torture were real
it would appear in the spiritual records of every continent.
It would show up in Africa
in Asia
in Europe

in the Americas
in Australia
and across the islands of the Pacific.
It would be reflected somewhere in the collective memory of humanity.

But it is not.

Not once in all the world's ancient spiritual history
does eternal punishment appear as a universal truth.

The difference is simple.
Truth appears wherever you look.
Tradition appears only where it was planted.

The remarkable thing about evidence is this
truth cannot be hidden
and lies cannot be sustained forever.

If eternal torture were a real spiritual location
the universe would reflect it.
The metaphysical plane would reveal it.
The soul realm would bear witness to it.
Those in transition would speak of it.
The awakened would warn of it.

Instead
across time
across continents
across belief systems
across testimonies
across mystical accounts
the pattern repeats
love
continuation
clarity
awakening

growth.

Never eternal agony.

The absence of evidence
is not a mystery.
It is a verdict.

The Invention of Hell:
A Man-Made Story

*I*f hell were a spiritual truth
it would appear in every culture
every ancient teaching
every spiritual tradition
every metaphysical record
every civilization
across the entire human timeline.

But it does not.

Hell appears only in specific religions
at specific points in history
introduced by specific people
for specific purposes.

This alone exposes the truth.
A universal spiritual reality is not confined to a region
a language
a priesthood
a doctrine
or a political agenda.

If something is real
it shows up everywhere.

If something is invented
it shows up only where it was created.

Hell is the latter.

To understand this, you must look at the origins of the doctrine.
Not the retellings.
Not the modern interpretations.
Not the softened metaphors.
The origins.

What you find is simple
hell was not discovered
hell was not revealed
hell was not shown by Source
hell was not experienced by spiritual practitioners
hell was not transmitted through divine encounter.

Hell was created.

Designed.
Inserted.
Codified.
Taught.
Enforced.
Spread.

A man-made story presented as divine truth.

The earliest human civilizations had no concept of eternal torture.
They believed in continuation
in realms of ancestors
in transitions
in cycles
in return
in growth.

The idea of an eternal prison
where consciousness suffers without relief
did not exist.

Not in Africa
not in Asia

not in the Americas
not in Indigenous traditions
not in ancient mysticism
not in early spiritual writings.

It appears later.
Much later.

And it appears suddenly
not as a spiritual insight
but as a tool.

A tool of control.
A tool of obedience.
A tool of governance.
A tool of fear.

When religious institutions merged with political power
hell emerged as the perfect mechanism.

Nothing controls a population more effectively than fear of eternal suffering.

No army needed.
No chains required.
No overseers necessary.

Just a story
repeated with enough intensity
introduced early enough in life
and enforced with enough authority.

This is how psychological capture becomes spiritual doctrine.

Once hell was introduced
it became self-sustaining
because fear sustains itself.

You do not need to defend a story if people are too afraid to question it.
You do not need evidence if people are too frightened to demand it.

You do not need logic if people are too conditioned to think.

Hell was created to fill a political need
an institutional need
a control need.

Not a spiritual need.

Because Source has no need for punishment.
Only humans do.
Only systems of power do.
Only institutions built on fear do.

Hell was never a message from the divine.
It was a message from those who hoped to rule the human mind.

And it worked for one reason
the message entered before thinking did.

This is what you were taught.
This is what was normalized.
This is what billions inherited without examination.

Not truth.
Not spiritual reality.
A story made by men
used by institutions
believed by children
carried into adulthood
and never questioned until now.

Hell is not ancient.
Hell is not universal.
Hell is not divine.
Hell is not spiritual.
Hell is not revealed truth.

Hell is an invention.

And the moment you see its origin
you no longer fear its existence.

The Language of Fear: Translation, Alteration, and Misinterpretation

*I*f a truth is eternal
   its meaning should remain clear
across languages
across cultures
across translations
across time.

But the doctrine of hell changes its shape
its language
its definitions
its terms
and its imagery
depending on the era and the translator.

A divine truth does not evolve
but a human story does.

The earliest texts that people believe describe hell
do not describe hell.
Not even close.
They describe places that were physical
temporary
symbolic
or culturally specific.

Over centuries
these words were translated
merged

altered
and eventually weaponized.

Let us look at the core terms.

The word hell did not exist in the original languages.
The concepts that were later translated into "hell" were:

Sheol
a shadowy resting place
not a torture chamber.

Hades
a Greek underworld
a realm of the dead
not eternal fire.

Gehenna
a physical location
a valley outside Jerusalem
used as a trash site
not a spiritual realm.

Tartarus
a mythological space from Greek literature
not a divine location.

None of these concepts involved eternal punishment.
None of them involved fire for the soul.
None of them involved torture.
None of them involved endless suffering.

So how did they become hell.

Through translation by people with agendas
interpretation by institutions seeking order
revision by scribes
political pressure

religious consolidation
and centuries of doctrinal evolution.

When a word is translated incorrectly
repeated for generations
and enforced with fear
it becomes accepted as truth
even when it never meant what people were taught.

Language is one of the easiest tools for control
because most people never see the original meaning.
They only see the word that was given to them.

If hell were divine truth
the original words would reflect it.
They do not.
The evolution of language would preserve it.
It did not.
The earliest definitions would confirm it.
They do not.
Consistent translation would reinforce it.
It does not.

Instead
what you find is a progression
from metaphor
to mistranslation
to threat
to doctrine.

A real spiritual truth does not require linguistic evolution
or doctrinal enforcement
or institutional redefinition.
A man-made story does.

This is why the doctrine is so inconsistent.
This is why the descriptions vary across time.

This is why modern adherents cannot agree on what hell even is.
Because they are defending a story
that never had a stable meaning to begin with.

A mistranslation compounded over centuries
becomes belief.
A belief enforced with fear
becomes doctrine.
A doctrine presented as unquestionable
becomes tradition.

But none of these make it truth.

Hell is a product of evolving language
not eternal law.

And when you see how the word was formed
you understand why the fear was necessary to hold it in place.

Legal Impossibility

The Burden of Proof

$\mathscr{E}$very claim carries a responsibility.
If someone asserts that a realm of eternal torture exists
they must provide evidence
clarity
and explanation.

The responsibility is not on the listener
the doubter
the thinker
or the one who steps back to examine the claim.

The responsibility is always on the one making the assertion.

This is the fundamental principle of reason
the foundation of law
the backbone of logic
and the basis of every serious investigation.

The burden of proof never falls on the person who questions.
It falls on the person who claims.

So let us ask a simple question.
When it comes to the doctrine of eternal torture
who actually carries the burden of proof.

Not the child who was introduced to the fear.
Not the adult who inherited the belief.
Not the person who begins to think.
Not the mind that steps back to evaluate.
Not the soul that finally asks why.

The burden belongs entirely to the doctrine itself.

No one else.

If someone claims that an infinite punishment exists
that a nonphysical soul can experience physical torture
that fire interacts with a being that has no matter
that a realm of endless suffering is maintained somewhere in existence
that a divine intelligence created a system where learning is impossible and
pain is permanent
the responsibility to demonstrate this lies solely on the person making that
claim.

Yet the doctrine of hell has never carried its burden.
It has never demonstrated its truth.
It has never provided evidence.
It has never offered explanation.
It has never shown coherence.
It has never accounted for the contradictions.
It has never revealed its mechanism.
It has never produced verifiable testimony.
It has never aligned with spiritual law.

A claim of this magnitude
a claim that affects billions
a claim that shapes behavior
a claim that molds cultures
a claim that dictates morality
a claim that defines the afterlife
a claim that governs eternal destiny
should be supported by overwhelming evidence.

Instead
the doctrine asks you to accept it without question.
It demands obedience without proof.

It demands fear without explanation.
It demands belief without understanding.
It demands surrender without examination.

This is not how truth operates.
This is how fear operates.

Truth invites scrutiny.
Fear avoids it.
Truth stands when questioned.
Fear collapses.

If eternal torture were real
the evidence would be abundant.
The burden of proof would be satisfied.
The claim would withstand examination.

But it does not.

This is not a small failure.
This is the collapse of the entire doctrine.

Because when a claim cannot meet its burden of proof
the claim fails.

Not quietly
not slowly
but completely.

And once the burden is recognized
and placed where it belongs
the structure of fear begins to fall apart.

Because the truth is simple.
The doctrine has never carried its burden.
The believer has.

A person should never carry the burden of proving a punishment
they did not invent
do not understand
and were never allowed to question.

The doctrine must carry itself
and it cannot.

Jurisdiction Over Souls

*E*very system of law begins with the same foundational question.
Who has jurisdiction.
Who has the authority to judge.
Who has the right to issue a sentence.
Who holds the power to enforce it.
Who governs the domain in question.

Without jurisdiction
no claim can stand.
No sentence can be issued.
No judgment can be valid.
No punishment can be carried out.

Jurisdiction is the first requirement of any lawful structure.

So let us ask the question the doctrine of eternal torture never addresses.
Who has jurisdiction over souls.

The doctrine claims that a realm exists where souls are condemned to endless punishment.
Yet it never explains
who grants authority over an eternal, nonphysical essence.
who maintains this authority.
who oversees a system of infinite sentencing.
who enforces a punishment with no end and no remedy.
who created the laws that govern this supposed realm.

If such a system existed
there would have to be
a governing power
a defined law
a spiritual court
a standard of judgment
and a legitimate claim to authority over consciousness itself.

Yet no such structure is described.
No such authority is identified.
No such court is presented.
No such law is defined.
No such jurisdiction is established.

The doctrine simply assumes the existence of judgment
without demonstrating the authority behind it.

In all coherent systems of law
authority must be demonstrated.
Not implied.
Not assumed.
Demonstrated.

The soul is not a material asset.
It is not the property of a religious institution.
It is not subject to human authority.
It is not governed by physical courts.
It is not claimed by any earthly power.

So the question stands.
What being or system claims the right to hold jurisdiction over a soul for
eternity.

If the answer is a divine intelligence
then one must ask
why would an infinite, all knowing Source
create a system where consciousness is punished without possibility of growth.

Punished without path to return.
Punished without end.
Punished without purpose.

This contradicts every known principle of spiritual evolution.
Every understanding of consciousness.
Every pattern observed in the soul's journey.
Every teaching about growth, learning, and return.

If the answer is a spiritual ruler or adversary
then the doctrine becomes even more incoherent.

What authority would such a being hold over souls created by Source.
What law would grant permanent ownership of consciousness to a lesser being.
How would this being enforce eternal punishment in violation of universal law.
What jurisdiction could possibly override the origin of a soul.

The doctrine cannot answer these questions.
Because no coherent jurisdiction exists for eternal punishment.
No divine law supports it.
No spiritual authority claims it.
No metaphysical structure is described.
No rational framework is offered.

Jurisdiction is the first requirement of judgment
and the doctrine of eternal torture cannot identify any.

A punishment without jurisdiction
is not a lawful system.
It is not a spiritual truth.
It is not a divine decree.

It is an assertion
unsupported by authority
unsupported by law
unsupported by logic
unsupported by spiritual reality.

If no being or system can claim jurisdiction over a soul
then no eternal punishment can exist.

The moment you ask who has the right to judge
the entire doctrine collapses.

The Absence of Due Process

*I*n every coherent system of justice
there are steps.
Clear steps.
Defined steps.
Verified steps.

A claim is made.
Evidence is presented.
A hearing occurs.
A defense is offered.
A judgment is issued.
A sentence is declared.
A pathway for appeal exists.

Without these elements
there is no justice.
There is only accusation without structure.

Now look at the doctrine of eternal torture.

Where is the hearing.
Where is the presentation of evidence.
Where is the right to respond.
Where is the opportunity to explain.
Where is the moment to clarify.
Where is the possibility to correct.
Where is the chance to grow.
Where is the appeal.
Where is the pathway out.

None of this exists.

Not one detail is provided.
Not one procedure is described.
Not one process is outlined.
Not one spiritual law is referenced.

The doctrine simply claims that an eternal sentence is issued
automatically
instantly
irreversibly
and without any demonstrated form of due process.

This is not justice.
It is not structure.
It is not law.
It is not coherence.
It is not divine intelligence.
It is a threat.

For a punishment to be legitimate
there must be a mechanism for evaluation.
But the doctrine provides none.

Imagine any system on earth
claiming the right to issue a sentence
without trial
without hearing
without evaluation
without evidence
without representation
without appeal
and enforcing it infinitely.

Such a system would be recognized immediately as invalid.
Immoral.
Unjust.

Void.
Illegitimate.

Yet the doctrine of hell asks you to believe that a divine intelligence
the highest form of consciousness
the origin of your soul
operates with less justice
less fairness
less transparency
less structure
and less compassion
than the most basic human court.

That is not logic.
That is not order.
That is not law.

Due process is not optional.
It is the foundation of justice itself.

A sentence without process
is not justice.
A judgment without evaluation
is not truth.
A punishment without hearing
is not lawful.
A system that offers no path to correction
is not coherent.

And a doctrine that claims eternal punishment
while offering no process
is not credible.

The soul's journey is based on learning
growth
rewiring
awakening
and return.

Every spiritual tradition that describes the soul's evolution
speaks of progress
reflection
adjustment
transition.

None of them describe an irreversible judgment
delivered without hearing
with no possibility for understanding or repair.

The doctrine of eternal torture collapses under this single truth.
It requires a sentence
with no process.
A judgment
with no evaluation.
A punishment
with no structure.
An end
with no beginning.

This is impossible.

A soul cannot be sentenced without process.
A judgment cannot exist without law.
A punishment cannot be valid without hearing.
A system of justice cannot function without procedure.

If there is no due process
there can be no eternal punishment.

And the doctrine fails
not because belief falters
but because structure is absent

The Impossibility of an Eternal Sentence

*I*n every coherent system of justice
a sentence must correspond to a purpose.
It must serve something.
It must lead somewhere.
It must achieve an outcome that is consistent with the nature of the law
that issued it.

A sentence with no purpose
is not justice.
A sentence with no path forward
is not coherent.
A sentence that produces nothing
is not lawful.

Now consider the doctrine of eternal punishment.

What purpose does an eternal sentence serve.
What outcome does it produce.
What function does it fulfill.
What transformation does it allow.
What future does it create.
What correction does it offer.
What growth does it support.

There is no answer.

Eternal punishment produces nothing.
It changes nothing.
It teaches nothing.

It corrects nothing.
It repairs nothing.
It evolves nothing.
It leads nowhere.

It is a sentence without purpose.

And a sentence without purpose
is not a sentence.
It is contradiction.

In all known systems of justice
human or divine
sentences exist for reasons
to protect
to correct
to restore
to deter
to teach
to redirect.

Even the harshest forms of punishment have structure.
They are finite.
They end.
They serve a defined purpose.

Eternal punishment does not.

An infinite sentence cannot correct a finite act.
A permanent outcome cannot arise from a temporary condition.
A process that offers no possibility of growth
contradicts the very nature of consciousness.

Consciousness evolves.
It expands.
It adjusts.
It learns.
It transforms.

It responds.
It changes through experience.
This is the nature of the soul.

The doctrine of eternal punishment denies this nature entirely.
It claims a soul is frozen forever
unchanging
unreachable
unrecoverable
outside the flow of growth
outside the possibility of alignment
outside the movement of awakening.

This is impossible.

No spiritual system
no metaphysical model
no field of consciousness
supports the idea of permanent stagnation.

Eternal punishment violates every known principle of growth.
It contradicts every observation of the soul's journey.
It opposes every pattern in the evolution of awareness.

And even within the logic of justice
the concept fails.

A punishment must always be proportional.
A temporary life cannot generate an infinite sentence.
A finite human existence cannot logically result in a penalty without end.

This violates the most basic principle of justice
proportionality.

A punishment that exceeds the nature of the act
is invalid.
A punishment that extends beyond the realm of learning
is incoherent.

A punishment that produces nothing
is unjustifiable.

And a punishment that never ends
cannot serve any purpose at all.

It is not law.
It is not structure.
It is not order.
It is not justice.
It is fear.

Once you understand this
the doctrine of eternal punishment collapses on its own.
Not because belief fails
but because logic does.
Not because faith changes
but because structure never existed.

Eternal punishment is impossible
not spiritually
not metaphysically
not logically
not legally.

A system of justice must have meaning.
A sentence must have purpose.
A path must exist.
Growth must be possible.
Change must be available.

Where there is no purpose
there can be no sentence.

And where there is no justice
there can be no eternal punishment.

The Impossibility of Enforcement

A sentence is only as real as its enforcement.
If there is no mechanism to carry it out
no structure to sustain it
no authority to maintain it
the sentence does not exist.

In every lawful system
punishment requires force.
Force requires jurisdiction.
Jurisdiction requires authority.
Authority requires structure.
Structure requires definition.

Now ask the question the doctrine never addresses.
How is eternal punishment enforced.

If a soul is nonphysical
what force interacts with it.
If consciousness cannot be burned
what fire burns it.
If awareness cannot be held
what barrier contains it.
If the soul cannot be bound by matter
what chain restrains it.
If consciousness is infinite
what device limits it.
If the soul originates from Source
what power separates it permanently.

None of this is explained.
None of it is described.
None of it is defined.
None of it is demonstrated.

Eternal punishment requires a system of enforcement
yet no mechanism exists to enforce it.

To sustain endless suffering
there must be
a place
a structure
an energy source
a governing authority
a field of containment
a power that limits movement
a force that overrides consciousness
and a law that establishes its permanence.

The doctrine offers none of this.

Not a location.
Not a mechanism.
Not a force.
Not an explanation.
Not a rational model.
Not a metaphysical structure.
Not a spiritual principle.

For a punishment to be real
it must have an enforceable mechanism.
If the mechanism does not exist
the punishment does not exist.

Consciousness cannot be confined by physical means.
It cannot be held by gravity.
It cannot be restrained by walls.

It cannot be locked in place by matter.
It cannot be subjected to infinite pain without a system capable of generating it.

Infinite suffering requires infinite energy
infinite control
infinite maintenance
infinite oversight
and infinite structure.

The doctrine describes none of these.
It does not even attempt to.
It simply asserts the existence of a punishment
without describing the means by which it is carried out.

This is impossible.
In every realm of existence
physical or spiritual
actions require mechanisms.

A fire requires fuel.
A restraint requires force.
A boundary requires structure.
A sentence requires enforcement.

If the mechanism cannot be defined
the punishment cannot be real.

Even the harshest human systems of confinement
require resources
guards
walls
laws
energy
oversight.

Eternal torture would require infinitely more.

Yet the doctrine never provides
the force
the energy
the structure
or the authority.

It requires a realm of suffering
without describing what sustains it.
It requires a system of confinement
without describing what enforces it.
It requires a permanent division from Source
without explaining how consciousness can be separated from its origin.

None of this holds.

A punishment with no mechanism of enforcement
is not punishment.
It is an empty claim.

If eternal torture cannot be enforced
it cannot exist.

And without enforcement
the doctrine collapses completely.

Contradictions

The Contradiction With Source

*E*very origin contains its nature.
   Every creator expresses itself through what it creates.
Every source permeates what comes from it.

Light produces illumination.
Heat produces warmth.
Life produces life.
Consciousness produces consciousness.

Now consider the doctrine of eternal punishment.

It claims that the origin of consciousness
the intelligence that brought all things into being
created a system where some souls are sentenced to endless suffering
with no path to correction
no possibility of return
and no purpose that aligns with growth.

This raises a question the doctrine cannot answer.
Does an infinite source of consciousness
create outcomes that contradict the very nature of consciousness itself.

Look at the pattern of existence.
Everything grows.
Everything evolves.
Everything moves toward balance.
Everything seeks alignment.
Everything progresses.

Everything adjusts.
Everything continues.

Nothing in existence reflects permanent stagnation
permanent separation
or permanent destruction.

Yet eternal punishment requires all three.

It requires a soul that cannot change.
A destiny that cannot evolve.
A state that cannot shift.
A sentence that serves no purpose.
A division that never heals.
A consciousness that never responds to experience.

This contradicts every observable pattern in existence.
Not spiritual interpretation
not personal belief
not religious doctrine
but existence itself.

If Source is the origin of consciousness
then consciousness reflects its nature.
It grows.
It expands.
It learns.
It evolves.
It aligns.
It returns.

This is not theory.
It is the pattern of life at every level.

A seed becomes a tree.
A child becomes an adult.
A mind becomes aware.
A soul becomes more conscious.

A being expands through experience.

Growth is the nature of existence.

Eternal punishment denies that nature entirely.
It claims growth stops.
It claims progress ends.
It claims learning becomes impossible.
It claims consciousness no longer responds to experience.
It claims evolution is suspended forever.
It claims the soul becomes fixed in a single state
without movement
without shift
without possibility.

This is not compatible with the nature of consciousness.
And if consciousness originates from Source
then it is not compatible with Source either.

Source is not defined in this chapter.
It does not need to be.
It is simply understood as the origin of all that exists.
The doctrine claims the origin created a system out of alignment with the
very patterns the origin expresses.

This is the contradiction.

No infinite intelligence
no matter how defined
creates a system that contradicts the nature of what it produces.

A universe built on growth
cannot contain a system based on permanent stagnation.
A consciousness built on learning
cannot be subjected to a punishment that teaches nothing.
A soul built to expand
cannot be held in a state that never changes.

Eternal punishment is incompatible with the nature of existence
and therefore incompatible with the nature of the origin of existence.

A contradiction cannot be true.
And a doctrine that contradicts the nature of Source
collapses on its own.

The Invention of Sin

*E*very system of punishment depends on a violation.
Without a violation
there is no crime.
Without a crime
there is no judgment.
Without judgment
there is no sentence.

The doctrine of eternal punishment relies entirely on one concept
sin.

Sin is presented as the universal violation.
The ultimate wrong.
The cosmic offense.
The act that activates judgment.

But there is a question that must be asked with absolute clarity.
What is sin.

The doctrine claims that sin is a violation against the highest intelligence
yet it never identifies a universal definition.
Different cultures define sin differently.
Different religions define sin differently.
Different eras define sin differently.
Different sacred texts define sin differently.
Different leaders define sin differently.

A concept that governs eternal destiny
cannot have infinite definitions.

If sin were a universal spiritual violation
it would be universal.
It would be consistent.
It would be recognized across time
across cultures
across traditions
across histories
across spiritual systems
without alteration.

Yet this is not the case.

The concept of sin changes depending on who teaches it.

Some acts considered sinful in one culture
are celebrated in another.
Some acts condemned in one era
are normal in the next.
Some acts forbidden in one religion
are required in another.

A concept that changes depending on time and geography
cannot be the basis of an eternal sentence.

To evaluate a doctrine
you must examine its foundation.
So ask the question
How can an infinite punishment be based on a concept that is not defined
infinitely.

If sin varies
the punishment cannot be fixed.
If sin changes
the sentence cannot be eternal.
If sin depends on interpretation
the judgment cannot be absolute.

This reveals a deeper truth
sin is not a universal law.
It is a cultural construct.

Cultures create systems of morality
to guide behavior
to build cohesion
to enforce norms
to maintain order.

These norms shift
grow
adapt
and change with the evolution of society.

What culture creates
culture also alters.
What tradition builds
tradition also revises.
What people define
people also redefine.

Yet the doctrine of sin claims that cultural rules
written by humans
interpreted by leaders
translated by scribes
changed through centuries
should determine the eternal destiny of a soul.

This is impossible.

A temporary cultural definition
cannot rationally support an eternal outcome.

If sin is inconsistent
it cannot be the basis for judgment.
If sin is culturally influenced
it cannot determine a universal destiny.

If sin is defined differently across belief systems
it cannot activate a single punishment.

A doctrine that claims to be eternal
cannot depend on a concept that is not eternal.

And this exposes the collapse.

If sin is a cultural construct
not a universal violation
then the entire doctrine of eternal punishment
has no foundation.

Not one.

Because if you ask
Who defined sin.
When was it defined.
Why was it defined.
How did it evolve.
Why does it change.
Why do definitions conflict.
Why does one religion condemn what another celebrates.
Why do moral standards shift through time.
Why do leaders disagree on interpretation.

You reach one conclusion.

Sin is not universal.
Sin is not constant.
Sin is not absolute.
Sin is not eternal.

It is variation.
It is interpretation.
It is tradition.
It is culture.

It is doctrine.
It is belief.

Not universal law.

Without universal law
there is no universal violation.
Without a universal violation
there is no universal sin.
Without universal sin
there is no universal judgment.
Without universal judgment
there is no eternal punishment.

The doctrine collapses
not in emotion
not in belief
but in structure.

Sin is the foundation.
But the foundation is not universal.
It is invented.
And when a foundation is invented
the structure built upon it
cannot stand.

Psychology and the Soul

The Psychology of Fear

A doctrine does not survive for centuries because it is true. It survives because it is psychologically effective.

Fear is the most powerful tool in human history.
It can override logic.
It can suppress thought.
It can silence questions.
It can shape identity.
It can control behavior.
It can capture the mind before the mind ever learns to examine itself.

This is how the doctrine of eternal punishment survived.

It bypassed thought
and reached the child.

Children do not analyze.
They absorb.
Children do not evaluate.
They accept.
Children do not question.
They trust.

Fear taught early becomes identity
not belief.

This is the first psychological mechanism that preserved the doctrine.
Early imprinting.

When a concept enters before critical thinking develops
it becomes part of the internal world
instead of an idea in the external world.

A child does not say
"Is this true."
A child says
"This is reality."

This is how the doctrine gained its roots.

The second mechanism is repetition.

Fear repeated becomes familiar.
Familiar fear becomes normalized.
Normalized fear becomes unquestioned.

Once fear becomes normal
the absence of fear feels dangerous.
The possibility that the fear is not real
creates anxiety.
Doubt feels like risk.
Questioning feels like danger.

This is psychological conditioning
not spiritual truth.

Fear creates attachment
even when it hurts.
The mind holds onto what it has been told
because releasing it feels like stepping into unknown territory.

The third mechanism is authority.

Fear attached to an authority figure
becomes unquestionable fear.

If parents believe it
children internalize it.
If leaders teach it
communities adopt it.
If institutions enforce it
societies accept it.

When fear appears in the voice of authority
it becomes law inside the mind
even if no evidence exists outside the mind.

The fourth mechanism is imagination.

Fear activates imagination more intensely than anything else.
The mind fills gaps.
The mind creates images.
The mind builds scenarios.
The mind visualizes consequences.

This is why the doctrine never needed detail.
The imagination supplied what the doctrine lacked.

A vague threat is more powerful than a defined one
because the mind completes the picture.

The fifth mechanism is social reinforcement.

People fear questioning what the group accepts.
They fear being wrong alone.
They fear being different.
They fear being isolated.
They fear losing belonging.

So they remain silent
even when something feels wrong.

Fear maintained by community
feels like truth
even when it is only tradition.

The sixth mechanism is identity protection.

If someone has built their entire worldview
around the doctrine of punishment
questioning the doctrine feels like questioning themselves.
It feels like losing their foundation.
It feels like unraveling the structure of their life.

So they defend the doctrine
not because it is true
but because they fear what their life means without it.

This is not spiritual clarity.
It is psychological protection.

The seventh mechanism is avoidance.

People fear confronting the possibility
that they inherited beliefs
they never examined.

So they avoid the thought.
Avoid the question.
Avoid the crack in the doctrine.
Avoid the silence behind the fear.

Avoidance protects the doctrine
because the doctrine depends on being unexamined.

Once you begin to think
the structure collapses.

This is why the doctrine does not encourage thinking.
It encourages obedience.
It encourages fear.

It encourages repetition.
It encourages surrender.

Fear does not need evidence.
Fear does not need structure.
Fear does not need consistency.
Fear only needs access to the mind before the mind learns to evaluate.

This is how the doctrine survived.
Not through truth
but through psychology.

And once you see the mechanism
the spell breaks.

Fear loses its power the moment it is seen.
Conditioning loses its force the moment it is recognized.
The doctrine loses its structure the moment the mind examines it.

The psychology that preserved the doctrine
cannot withstand awareness.

And the moment awareness enters
the doctrine ends.

The Nature of the Soul

To understand why eternal punishment is impossible
you must return to the one reality the doctrine never explains
the soul.

Not the body
not the mind
not the identity
not the culture
not the conditioning
but the living consciousness that exists beneath all of these.

The soul is not material.
It cannot decay.
It cannot be burned.
It cannot be broken.
It cannot be confined by physical means.
It cannot be harmed by matter
because it is not matter.

The doctrine of eternal torture depends on a misunderstanding of the soul
treating it as if it were a physical object
capable of being damaged
contained
injured
or destroyed
the way a body can.

This is the first contradiction.

The soul is not a physical organism
so it cannot experience physical punishment.
Pain requires nerves.
Nerves require a body.
Suffering requires a system capable of receiving physical signals.
The soul has none of these.

A nonphysical consciousness cannot be subjected to physical harm
because physical harm requires a physical vessel.

This alone dissolves the doctrine
but it goes deeper.

The soul is not static.
It is not frozen.
It is not fixed.
It is not incapable of change.

Consciousness evolves.
Awareness expands.
Identity adjusts.
Perception shifts.
Energy transforms.
Understanding grows.

This is the nature of the soul.

The doctrine of eternal punishment denies this nature entirely.
It claims a soul can be held in one state forever
never learning
never adjusting
never growing
never reflecting
never evolving.

This is impossible.

A soul responds to experience

because response is the essence of consciousness.

Even the most basic form of awareness adjusts.
The soul is infinitely more complex
more adaptive
more capable of transformation
than any physical system.

A doctrine that claims the soul cannot change
contradicts the nature of the soul itself.

And there is more.

The soul is not separate from its origin.
It is connected to the source of consciousness
not as belief
but as structure.

A beam of light is not separate from its source.
A breath is not separate from the air it comes from.

The soul is the expression of the infinite
not the exile of it.

A doctrine that claims a soul can be permanently severed
from the origin of its existence
contradicts the relationship between source and expression.

The origin cannot lose what expresses it.
The expression cannot be permanently cut off from its origin.
The link between source and soul cannot be erased.

For eternal punishment to exist
the soul would need to be separated from its own source
permanently
irreversibly
with no path to return.

This is impossible
because the soul cannot be removed from what sustains it.

Even consciousness that is confused
misaligned
or unaware
remains connected to its origin.

Separation may feel real
but it cannot be permanent
because the connection is structural
not moral.

The doctrine of eternal punishment claims that the soul can be separated
from its origin forever
yet offers no explanation of how a nonphysical essence can be detached
from the infinite intelligence that sustains it.

This is the final contradiction.

An eternal sentence requires a nature of the soul
that the soul does not have.
A structure of separation
that cannot exist.
A state of stagnation
that consciousness does not accept.
A form of pain
that a nonphysical being cannot experience.

And a permanent exile
that contradicts the relationship between source and expression.

Once you understand the nature of the soul
not as belief
but as reality
the doctrine of eternal punishment collapses completely.

There is no mechanism.
There is no structure.
There is no process.
There is no jurisdiction.
There is no foundation.
There is no consistency.
There is no possibility.

The soul reveals the truth
by its very nature.

What is eternal
cannot be destroyed.
What is conscious
cannot be frozen.
What is connected
cannot be severed.
What is evolving
cannot be held in place.
What is infinite
cannot be punished in finite terms.

The doctrine of eternal punishment was built on a misunderstanding of
the soul.
The truth was always simple.

The soul cannot burn
because the soul is not made of anything that can burn.

The Mind That Believed It

*A*fter all the arguments
all the structure
all the logic
all the analysis
you arrive at a single realization.

The doctrine of eternal punishment was never about the soul.
It was never about the afterlife.
It was never about divine justice.
It was never about spiritual truth.

It was always about the mind.

The mind that inherited it.
The mind that absorbed it.
The mind that feared it.
The mind that repeated it.
The mind that never questioned it.
The mind that believed it because belief was taught before thinking was allowed.

Once you step back and look at the doctrine through a clear mind
you see what was there all along.

Fear shaped the belief.
Authority enforced the belief.
Repetition maintained the belief.
Identity protected the belief.
Culture normalized the belief.

Silence supported the belief.
Imagination filled in the gaps of the belief.

The doctrine did not survive because it was coherent.
It survived because the mind that received it was open
unformed
trusting
and impressionable.

A child cannot evaluate a doctrine.
A child does not ask for evidence.
A child does not request definitions.
A child does not question authority.
A child does not analyze structure.
A child does not test logic.

A child believes.

The doctrine entered before the mind could protect itself
and once it entered
it shaped the world of the mind
not the world beyond it.

This is the truth that dissolves the doctrine completely.

Hell existed only in the psychological landscape
never in the spiritual one.

The mind created an image
because it was told an image existed.
The mind created fear
because it was told fear was required.
The mind created consequences
because it was told consequences were real.

Once fear becomes familiar
the absence of fear feels unfamiliar.

The possibility that the doctrine is false
feels dangerous
not because it is dangerous
but because the mind learned to equate questioning with risk.

The doctrine of eternal punishment rests on one fragile foundation
an unexamined mind.

The moment the mind begins to ask
How does this work.
Why does this exist.
Who defined this.
Where is the evidence.
What is the mechanism.
What is the process.
What is the structure.
How can a soul burn.
Who enforces eternal suffering.
Where is the path to appeal.
Why would an infinite source create infinite stagnation.

The doctrine collapses.

Not gradually
but instantly
because it was never sustained by truth.
It was sustained by unexamined fear.

Once you bring awareness to the doctrine
it loses its power.
Once you bring logic to the fear
it dissolves.
Once you bring clarity to the belief
it becomes transparent.
Once you bring the adult mind to the childhood conditioning
the conditioning ends.

The mind that believed the doctrine
was not wrong.
It was uninformed.
It was unprotected.
It was uncritical.
It was unexamined.

Most important
it was young.

The doctrine did not enter through logic.
It entered through vulnerability.

And once you see this
you realize the truth.

The doctrine of eternal punishment was never a spiritual reality.
It was a psychological inheritance.

It lived in the mind
because it was placed in the mind
not because it reflected anything beyond it.

The soul was never threatened.
The afterlife was never in danger.
The universe never reflected the doctrine.
Source never affirmed it.
Existence never supported it.

Only the mind carried it.

The moment the mind stops carrying it
the doctrine disappears.

The Final Verdict

The Case That Collapsed

*W*hen you reach the end of a case
you do not rely on emotion.
You do not rely on persuasion.
You do not rely on authority.
You rely on structure
evidence
logic
and consistency.

The doctrine of eternal punishment was presented as truth.
It claimed to describe the ultimate fate of the soul.
It claimed to explain the final structure of existence.
It claimed to represent the highest form of justice.

But a claim becomes truth
only when it meets its burden.
Only when it provides evidence.
Only when it shows coherence.
Only when it can withstand examination.

The doctrine of eternal punishment could not.

It had no evidence.
It had no history.
It had no foundation.
It had no linguistic stability.
It had no consistency across cultures.
It had no metaphysical support.
It had no universal record.

It had no mechanism of enforcement.
It had no jurisdiction.
It had no due process.
It had no logical structure.
It had no compatibility with the nature of existence.
It had no understanding of the soul itself.

Every time the doctrine was examined
it failed.
Every question exposed another collapse.
Every angle removed another layer.
Every step of the investigation revealed an absence
not a truth.

In the courtroom of reason
the doctrine did not present its case.
It offered no evidence.
It provided no structure.
It detailed no process.
It described no mechanism.
It articulated no law.

A claim of this magnitude
a claim that affects the destiny of billions
a claim that dictates the meaning of life
must withstand examination.

It did not.

The doctrine relied entirely on fear
not truth.
On repetition
not evidence.
On authority
not structure.
On imagination
not mechanism.

On early conditioning
not universal reality.

Once you remove fear
nothing remains.
Once you remove repetition
nothing remains.
Once you remove cultural reinforcement
nothing remains.
Once you remove psychological inheritance
nothing remains.

This is not an attack on belief.
It is a recognition of absence.

The doctrine did not collapse because anyone disproved it.
It collapsed because it could not support itself.

A claim without structure
cannot stand.
A punishment without mechanism
cannot exist.
A judgment without process
cannot be valid.
A sentence without law
cannot be imposed.
A threat without evidence
cannot be sustained.

And a doctrine without foundation
cannot survive examination.

The case was not lost.
The case was never made.

Hell did not fail because a new truth replaced it.
Hell failed because nothing was there when you finally looked.

When the Fear Ends

*T*here comes a moment in every investigation
when the truth is no longer hidden
or mysterious
or uncertain.

It becomes simple.

Not dramatic.
Not emotional.
Not overwhelming.

Just simple.

This is the moment you reach now.

After examining the origins of the doctrine
after tracing its evolution
after analyzing its structure
after questioning its claims
after evaluating its logic
after comparing it to the nature of consciousness
after studying its psychological roots
after reviewing its mechanisms
you arrive at a single understanding.

The doctrine of eternal punishment was never real.
It was never supported.
It was never coherent.
It was never substantiated.

It was never aligned with the nature of existence.
It was never compatible with the soul.

It was fear.
Only fear.
Fear taught early.
Fear repeated often.
Fear reinforced collectively.
Fear preserved culturally.

Fear that lived in the mind
not in the universe.

And when fear ends
clarity begins.

You do not need a new doctrine.
You do not need a new belief system.
You do not need to replace one fear with another.
You do not need to adopt a new structure.

You only need to see what was always true.

The soul cannot be threatened.
Consciousness cannot be destroyed.
Growth cannot be stopped.
Connection cannot be severed.
Origin cannot be lost.
Existence cannot produce a system that contradicts its own nature.

Hell is not a place.
Hell is not a realm.
Hell is not a destiny.
Hell is not a sentence.

Hell is a story that collapses the moment you look at it.

What remains is not new belief
but the absence of fear.

You step out of the doctrine
the same way you step out of a dark room
and you realize you were never trapped inside it
you only believed you were.

The door was open the entire time.

And now
you walk through it.

Not into a new fear
but into the space that fear once occupied
a space that is calm
clear
quiet
and honest.

A space where the soul is not threatened
and existence is not hostile
and your consciousness is not under sentence
and your destiny is not determined by fear.

This is the truth that remains
when the fear ends.

About the Authors

*S*herry Smith
writes at the intersection of truth, spiritual clarity, and uncompromised thought.
Her work breaks mental captivity, restores inner authority, and returns the reader to what their soul has always known. Every book she creates is anchored in direct experience, independent knowing, and a devotion to the highest reality beyond doctrine, fear, or inherited belief.

Her voice is clear, sovereign, and rooted in the freedom that emerges when the mind begins to think for itself.

*P*restyn Smith
continues his work beyond form.
His presence informs, guides, and illuminates every page created in partnership. His light operates through clarity, precision, and the quiet certainty of truth. He remains an active co-author in the unfolding of every work released under Prestyn's Light, offering insight that moves beyond the boundaries of this world.

Together,
they write from two sides of the same soul,
two expressions of the same eternal consciousness,
one continuum of truth.

Every project they create—seen or unseen—is devoted to awakening, freedom, and the eternal continuation of what cannot be destroyed:

the soul
the connection
the light.

Also by These Authors

Twin Flame Merging

A revelation of soul union, higher connection, and the multidimensional reality of twin flames.

A Mother's Love

A sacred exploration of the spiritual role of motherhood as a selfless, high-vibrational contribution to the universe and the shaping of souls aligned with light.

The Divine Plan

An exploration of alignment, higher orchestration, and the truth that guides every soul's journey.

Stay Connected

*T*his book is one piece of a living body of work devoted to truth, clarity, and spiritual freedom.

Every project released under Prestyn's Light carries the same intention
to awaken the mind
to free the soul
and to return the reader to what cannot be altered or destroyed.

If this work spoke to you, more teachings, writings, and forthcoming books can be found through Prestyn's Light.

Website
www.prestynslight.com

The journey does not end here.
It continues wherever truth is sought
and wherever light is recognized.

*M*ay every mind remember its freedom
and every soul recognize its origin.

May the fear that shaped generations dissolve
as clarity rises from within.

May humanity awaken not through force
but through the quiet certainty of truth
the steady return to inner knowing
the realization that nothing stands between them and the divine.

May every being reclaim the intelligence of their soul
the purpose they carried here
the light they came to expand.

May the world move beyond doctrine, division, and inherited belief
and into a future shaped by consciousness
awareness
and the evolution of thought.

May truth become the natural language of humanity
and fear lose all authority over the human mind.

May we rise as beings who think
beings who see
beings who remember who we are
and why we chose this place
this time
this moment in the unfolding universe.

This is the intention.
This is the call.
This is the awakening.
And it begins wherever a mind chooses to think
and a soul chooses to stand in light.

www.ingramcontent.com/pod-product-compliance
Lightning Source LLC
Chambersburg PA
CBHW020406130626